AMERICA PREPARES FOR WAR

by

Wallace B. Black
and
Jean F. Blashfield

CRESTWOOD HOUSE

New York

Collier Macmillan Canada
Toronto

Maxwell Macmillan International Publishing Group
New York Oxford Singapore Sydney

Library of Congress Cataloging-in-Publication Data

Black, Wallace B.
    America Prepares for War/ by Wallace B. Black and Jean F. Blashfield. – 1st ed.
        p.   cm. – (World War II 50th anniversary series)
    Summary: Describes how and to what extent the United States was involved in World War II, including military preparation, before the United States actually declared war.
    ISBN 0-89686-554-1
    1. World War, 1939-1945 – United States – Juvenile literature.
2. United States – History – 1933-1945 – Juvenile literature.
[1. World War, 1939-1945 – United States.] I. Blashfield, Jean F. II. Title.
III. Series: Black, Wallace B. World War II 50th anniversary series.
D769.B47 1991
940.53'73–dc20

               90-46581
               CIP
               AC

Created and produced by B and B Publishing, Inc.

Picture Credits

Archives of Labor & Current Affairs, Wayne State University - page 22
Bittman Archives - page 24
Imperial War Museum - page 34
National Archives - pages 3, 5, 7, 8, 12, 20, 23, 25, 27, 29, 30, 33, 42, 43, 44
Office of War Information - page 19
United States Navy - pages 11, 17, 26, 28, 31, 32, 35, 45
United States Air Force - pages 15, 36, 37, 38, 39, 41
Steve Sullivan - Map - page 40

CRESTWOOD HOUSE

Macmillan Publishing Company
866 Third Avenue
New York, NY 10022

Collier Macmillan Canada, Inc.
1200 Eglinton Avenue East
Suite 200
Don Mills, Ontario M3C 3N1

Printed in the United States of America

First Edition

10 9 8 7 6 5 4 3 2 1

CONTENTS

Chapter 1

BETWEEN THE WARS

World War I ended in November of 1918. The United States had helped England, France and Russia defeat Germany. That was supposed to have been "the war to end all wars." The American people were glad it was over. They wanted to return to peace and a good life. The victorious army returned home in glory. The soldiers and sailors hurried to get back to their families and their jobs.

Life returned to normal. The Roaring Twenties, as the years from 1920 to 1930 were called, was a happy time. Businesses were booming. Everyone wanted "a car in every garage and a chicken in every pot."

With no war to fight, the military forces were soon cut back in size. But the Army Air Corps, founded during World War I, was active. General Billy Mitchell proved that land-based bombers could sink a battleship. Other heroic American aviators flew around the world. Even so, the army and navy rapidly drifted back to peacetime activities.

The average American liked the exciting "show-business" side of aviation. "Lucky" Charles Lindbergh was the first person to fly nonstop across the Atlantic Ocean. However, using airplanes for war was far from the minds of most Americans. They were sure that war would never come to America. Thousands of miles of oceans protected the United States from overseas enemies.

By 1929 everything seemed wonderful. Most Americans had plenty of money to spend. The world was at peace.

But all was not as it seemed. In Europe the Germans

After years of struggle, the German people were beginning to rebuild their country under Adolf Hitler. A powerful new army was part of Hitler's plans.

were having a difficult time rebuilding their country after the war. Their money was worthless. They felt themselves left out of the world. They started listening to a new leader, Adolf Hitler. He saw more war as an answer to his nation's problems.

Bad times were coming . . . the drums of war were beginning to be heard once again.

Chapter 2

WORLDWIDE PROBLEMS

In the fall of 1929 the American stock market crashed. Suddenly prosperity ended. Many people who owned stocks and bonds found that their shares were worthless. They were broke.

Within the next few years, thousands of businesses failed. Millions of people lost their jobs. Banks closed. The long period of American business failure, called the Depression, was felt around the world.

During the Depression even less money was spent on the United States military than before. The navy was still one of the most powerful in the world and the Army Air Corps had made some advances. But with little money to spend, the U.S. armed forces quickly became second-rate.

Germany and Japan

In Europe recovery from World War I was slow. The unhappy German people began to follow Adolf Hitler. Hitler was rebuilding Germany through the National Socialist, or Nazi, party. He promised Germans a great future. He said a new Germany would be built through military strength and new wealth. The wealth would come from other countries that he thought ought to belong to Germany. He particularly looked toward Austria, Czechoslovakia and Poland and all their land and natural resources.

The French watched these changes in their former enemy and became afraid that Germany might attack them again. They, too, began to rebuild their military forces. The French were afraid that Germany would try to become

*Adolf Hitler led the people of Germany from poverty to prosperity . . .
and finally to war.*

superpowerful again. The seeds of war were being planted once more.

Germany began to violate the terms of the Treaty of Versailles. That treaty, signed at the end of World War I, was supposed to keep Germany from rearming. But the Nazis ignored the treaty and began to build new machines of war. The League of Nations—an earlier version of the United Nations—did not have enough power to stop them.

Italy was also reaching out for new territory. Under the leadership of Benito Mussolini, it was taking over Ethiopia and other African territory. Like Germany, Italy was building a giant war machine.

On the other side of the world, another great military power was growing. Japan, a crowded island nation, needed more room for its many people. It also needed more food, coal and oil to support a growing population. The Japanese started to build a huge army, navy and air force. In 1932 Japan invaded Manchuria in northeastern China. It was ready to use military force to take over more of China to get the land and resources it needed.

The U. S. Depression

In the United States, Franklin D. Roosevelt was elected president in 1932. The people hoped he could solve their

Japanese troops taking over another city in north China

serious economic problems. He started what was called the New Deal. Government and business tried to work together. Every effort was made to restore jobs and to put American business back in order. Military spending and thoughts of war were pushed aside. People were too busy trying to make ends meet.

Millions of men were out of work, so the government created the Civilian Conservation Corps. The CCC, as it was called, took unemployed young men and put them to work in the country. They built parks and camps, cleared forests and paved roads. In many cases army bases were repaired and used by the CCC.

The WPA, or Work Projects Administration, was also set up to create jobs for unemployed people. Thousands of buildings and bridges were constructed. Hundreds of thousands of miles of paved roads were built. And thousands of jobs were created for actors, artists and writers.

Other programs provided help for businesses and factories. Old businesses were assisted in rebuilding and new ones created, so that Americans could start working again. These efforts put many people back to work. Americans didn't know it, but such programs helped them prepare for the war that was to come.

Only a few Americans were well informed about the increased military activity in Europe. They urged greater military spending and warned of the threat of another war. But in the mid-1930s, most people thought they were safe from attack. Many of them refused to consider that America might ever become involved in another war. These people were called isolationists because they wanted to keep the United States isolated from other nations' problems. They wanted America to remain neutral—to have no part in foreign wars. Other people, called pacifists, were against war for any and all reasons. A Neutrality Act was passed by Congress in 1935 that was supposed to keep the United States out of war forever.

Chapter 3

GERMANY AND JAPAN ON THE MOVE

In 1936 Hitler's intentions became clear. Germany took over lands that it had lost at the end of World War I. No one tried to stop the German advance. Hitler claimed that the Germans needed room to expand. His armies rapidly took over Austria and parts of Czechoslovakia. Again, Britain and France objected but did nothing to stop him.

The German air force, called the Luftwaffe, even took part in the Spanish Civil War, fighting on the side of Francisco Franco. Franco believed that Spain should have just one leader, himself. The Germans participated to gain experience in actual war. Some Americans also fought in the Spanish Civil War, fighting on the other side, against Franco and the Germans.

America's Isolation

Many Americans frowned on these warlike activities. Government officials spoke out against Hitler. But most people wanted to remained isolated, or apart, from Europe. These isolationists insisted that Europe's problems were not America's problems.

They did not think that China's problems were America's either. Japan started a full-scale war with China in 1937. But most Americans paid little attention. At that time a U.S. gunboat, the *Panay,* was on patrol in China's Yangtze River. It was attacked and sunk by Japanese aircraft. Some people changed their minds about isolation

The gunboat USS Panay *sinking after it was attacked by Japanese planes. The* Panay *was patrolling the Yangtze River in China.*

and wanted to fight the Japanese. But not many.

Important American political, business and religious leaders preached isolation and neutrality. Charles Lindbergh visited Germany and other European countries. The aviator and hero was impressed by the huge army and air force being built by Germany. But he was sure that Germany was no danger to America. He continued to urge America to mind its own business.

At the same time, the German-American Bund came into being. This was a group of social clubs made up of Americans who had German ancestors. Popular in many big cities, these clubs supported Germany. They urged other citizens to remain neutral in European affairs. They also provided cover for German agents spying on American industry and defense.

Powerful newspapers such as the *Chicago Tribune* also demanded neutrality and isolation. Many leaders in Congress were completely against rearming America. Other leaders were convinced that the United States had to start rebuilding its military. The country was split right down the middle.

Meeting of the German-American Bund in Madison Square Garden in New York City. The background painting shows George Washington flanked by Nazi swastikas.

Finally many more Americans became truly alarmed. Certain facts became clear to them: Germany was mistreating the Jews. The Japanese were waging a cruel war against the Chinese people. The Italian dictator Benito Mussolini had invaded parts of Africa as well as the European country of Albania.

Then, on September 1, 1939, Germany attacked Poland. England and France had agreed to fight for Poland. For the people of Europe, this meant that World War II had begun. The United States remained officially neutral although its sympathy lay with Poland and the other countries soon to be attacked by Germany. The American people could not just stand by and watch their friends and allies from World War I suffer.

No Longer Neutral

After the invasion of Poland, Congress voted to cancel some parts of the Neutrality Act. Now the United States could furnish military material to countries at war. This was done mainly to help Great Britain. Military spending at home was also increased. Campaigns were started to get men to enlist in the armed forces—just in case the United States got involved. The FBI was alerted to watch for spies and attempts at sabotage by people working for the Germans, Italians or Japanese.

Although pacifists and isolationists argued against it, the United States began to rearm. By June 1940 France, Belgium, the Netherlands, Norway, Denmark and Luxembourg had been conquered by Germany. Great Britain stood alone against Hitler. In order to help Britain fight Hitler and China fight Japan, American defense industries had to grow. In July 1940 a $5 billion defense budget was passed.

America was at last preparing for war. People were going back to work. The Depression was over.

An event had occurred in November 1939 that few people knew about. Albert Einstein had written a letter to President Roosevelt. Einstein was a brilliant Jewish scientist who had left Germany and come to the United States several years earlier. He told the president of work that was being done in the field of atomic energy. He suggested that "splitting the atom" might have an important military use.

In complete secrecy Roosevelt started America's scientists working on the Manhattan Project. That project began the development of the weapon that would eventually end the war—the atomic bomb.

Chapter 4

EAGLE SQUADRON

America did not enter the war until the Japanese bombed Pearl Harbor on December 7, 1941. But American men and ships had been fighting for Great Britain even before that. After Germany invaded Poland, Great Britain and France declared war on Germany. They had promised to defend Poland.

French and British soldiers found themselves being beaten by the same German blitzkrieg ("lightning war") tactics that had smashed Poland. By June 1940 France had fallen into the hands of the Germans. British forces had retreated to the safety of the British Isles.

Hundreds of young Americans rushed to Canada and England to volunteer to help the British fight. These young men could have been in serious trouble because of their actions. By leaving the country to fight, they avoided the draft at home. They also violated the Neutrality Act, part of which was still in effect. It outlawed the participation of individuals in other nations' wars. American officials chose to ignore the actions of these enthusiastic volunteers.

Some of the thousands of Americans who went to Canada to join up were pilots. Great Britain needed pilots badly. Hundreds of fliers had been lost in the battles leading up to the fall of France. As a result, over 200 American pilots went to England and flew in the Royal Air Force (RAF) from 1940 to 1942. These American pilots were known as the Eagle Squadron.

In the fall of 1940 the RAF formed the Seven-One Squadron, which was the official name of the first Eagle Squadron. The American volunteers were commanded by British officers. Many Eagle Squadron pilots were quite young and inexperienced. They lied about being over 18 years old. They bragged about their flying skills, which were often not as good as they said. The RAF, badly in need of pilots, took them in spite of these faults. But the members of the Eagle Squadron learned fast and became a fighting team. They were soon flying British Hurricane and Spitfire fighter planes in combat.

The American volunteers in the Eagle Squadron fought as a part of the RAF for almost two years. Some of them shot down five or more enemy aircraft and became aces.

Members of the RAF Eagle Squadron watch as other "Eagles" fly by. This was a ceremony that marked the squadron's becoming part of the U.S. Air Force.

They were a brave and wild bunch. The small salary they received was not their reason for fighting. Instead, they flew, fought and died for the cause of freedom. Over one-third of these volunteers were killed in combat.

Soon several Eagle Squadrons were formed. They fought from bases in Great Britain during the Battle of Britain. One squadron was sent to Malta in the Mediterranean Sea. The American Eagles fought bravely as part of the RAF wherever they were stationed.

America entered the war in December 1941. The surviving Eagles exchanged their RAF blue uniforms for U.S. Air Force khaki. In September 1942 they were officially transferred to the United States Eighth Air Force.

They had served valiantly, fighting and dying alongside their British comrades in the cause of freedom.

Destroyers for Britain

As the world moved into war, the war at sea became very fierce. Because Great Britain is an island, it depends on ships to bring most of its food and materials. Germany knew that if it could cut off Britain's supplies, it could win the war. The German navy sank British merchant ships faster than the British workers could build new ones.

Britain turned to America for help. After World War I the U.S. Navy had put a huge fleet of vessels into storage – "in mothballs." The British people needed those ships.

The U.S. Navy started patrolling the western Atlantic right after the war started in 1939. German U-boats (submarines) and surface raiders were attacking British convoys. American ships were often part of these convoys that sailed in dangerous waters. The U.S. Navy was there to protect them as well as to help the British.

But the navy needed more bases in the Western Hemisphere beyond the United States. Britain and the United States reached an agreement: Britain got 50 old destroyers left over from World War I. In exchange America got the use

U.S. Navy seaplanes and a blimp patrol for German submarines above a convoy in the western Atlantic Ocean.

of British ports in Bermuda, the Caribbean Sea and in Canada. American ships and aircraft could now patrol more of the western Atlantic Ocean.

The U.S. Navy got the destroyers out of storage. The ships were cleaned up, repaired and rearmed. They were then turned over to the Royal Navy. Within just a few months, 50 valuable warships were helping Great Britain fight the battle of the Atlantic. British convoys could now have more protection from German U-boats.

Chapter 5

YOU'RE IN THE ARMY NOW!

The biggest need in preparing for war is people. On September 16, 1940, Congress saw that the United States could soon be at war. It passed the Selective Training and Service Act. That meant that for the first time since World War I, young men were required to serve in the army. They could be removed from school or their jobs and sent into the armed forces. However, there was still a feeling that the United States ought not to fight in other people's wars. The law said that the soldiers could serve only within the Western Hemisphere or on U.S. bases in other countries, such as those in the Philippine Islands.

So, in 1940, every American male between the ages of 21 and 35 had to sign up for military service. More than 6,000 draft boards handled the actual signing up of the men. About 16 million men registered and were given a number.

After the men registered, each one was sent a questionnaire to fill out and send to his local draft board. Based on his answers, each man was placed in one of four different classes. Only young men without family or other responsibilities or health problems were to be drafted. They were classified 1-A.

On October 29, 1940, a lottery was held at which the numbers of the first men to be drafted were drawn from a big glass bowl. Those men whose numbers were picked and who were classified 1-A were told to report to their local draft boards for induction into the armed forces. For about 900,000 unmarried young men this meant *"You're in the army now!"* These draftees were now GIs, which is

Secretary of War Henry L. Stimson drawing the first numbers for the Selective Service draft in 1940. Drafting young men to serve in the armed services was a major step in preparing for war.

short for "government issue." Many other men volunteered instead of being drafted.

A few months later members of the Army and Navy Reserves (trained military men who were not on active duty) were called up. On January 15, 1941, state National Guard units were also called to active duty in the army.

The men drafted had to serve in the army for one year. After that one year, they could return to their old jobs. However, before that year was up, Congress declared a state of emergency and extended the period of service to 18 months. Before those 18 months were up, the United States had declared war on Japan and Germany. On December 8, 1941, the time limit was removed. American soldiers were now in for the "duration"—in other words, for as long as the war lasted.

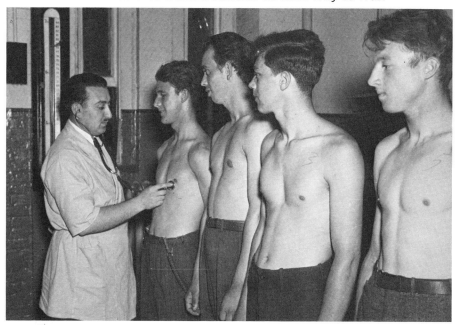

Inductees taking a physical exam after being drafted. Just a year later these same men would be trained soldiers on their way to war.

Chapter 6

CIVILIAN TO SOLDIER

The call to arms had been sent out. The United States had almost 2 million men signed up in the military by spring of 1941. They all had to be trained and equipped. Training bases were set up from coast to coast. Old equipment was brought out of storage. The factories of America were put to work day and night turning out new guns, ammunition and other military supplies.

But everything was still in short supply. The new recruits lived in tents until barracks to house them could be built. Sticks were sometimes used as rifles in basic training. In practice maneuvers when real tanks were not available, cars and trucks were used instead. They had signs on them that said THIS IS A TANK.

When Poland was invaded in September 1939 the U.S. Army had 464 outdated tanks. In 1940 production to supply tanks and trucks for Great Britain, Russia and the U.S. Army got under way. In 1941 about 12,000 tanks and trucks were built. By the time the war was over in 1945, America's war factories had built over 200,000 mechanized vehicles of all types.

As each day passed things got better. Army, navy and marine recruits received their basic training and were given needed equipment. Civilians became infantrymen, machine gunners, pilots, mechanics, mountaineers, sailors or marines within a few short months. The merchant marine (private shipping companies) and the Coast Guard were also busy. They were training the men needed to sail and protect the huge convoys of ships that were to carry goods between the United States, Great Britain, Russia and China.

Workers at a Chrysler plant prepare an M-3 tank for shipment to the army in early 1941.

Women in the War

Before the war the only American women in the armed forces were nurses in the Army and Navy Nurse Corps. A number of nurses were on active duty in the Philippine Islands when it fell to the Japanese in early 1942. They spent the entire war as prisoners.

As the war progressed women were brought into more

and more roles. The Women's Army Corps was founded in May 1942. Women soldiers, called WACs, did just about everything male soldiers did except serve in actual combat. Women joined the U.S. Navy two months later. They were called WAVEs. Women entered the Marine Corps the following February.

After the U. S. entered the war, famous pilots Jacqueline Cochran and Nancy Harkness Love started the Women Airforce Service Pilots, or WASPs. However, in early 1941 some women flew long hours ferrying airplanes from factories to army and navy bases in the United States. A few even flew bombers and transports to England where they were needed for combat.

As more men were drafted, women started taking men's places in business and industry. "Rosie the Riveter" became a symbol of all women who worked in heavy industry, where women had never worked before.

A riveter at work on an airplane at the Lockheed Aircraft factory. With men being drafted by the millions, women had to take their places in the nation's factories.

As early as 1941, women began ferrying aircraft from factories to army and navy bases in the U.S. Seen here is a group of women pilots heading for the flight line.

The New Pilots

President Roosevelt called for the training of 50,000 pilots. Flight training was started at colleges and universities around the country. Members of the Army Air Corps (as the air force was first called) and navy cadets received their primary flight training in schools operated by civilians. Many future fighter and bomber pilots got their first taste of flying in tiny Piper Cubs.

Basic and advanced flight training was given by the military. In just six months, successful cadets received 200 hours of flight training and about the same amount of ground school, where they learned about engines, weather, navigation and safety rules. They were then ready to go on to fighter or bomber training.

New aircraft were coming off the production lines more quickly every day. Pilots were not the only airmen to be trained. Thousands of navigators, mechanics and bombardiers were also being prepared to make up crews for the growing fleet of military aircraft. Before the end of the war almost 300,000 aircraft were produced and put into service.

Chapter 7

SUPPLYING AMERICA'S ALLIES

Starting with getting old ships in exchange for bases, Great Britain came to depend on the United States for needed supplies. British factories were being bombed and were not able to meet the country's needs.

Under the leadership of President Roosevelt, America gave full support to Great Britain. Every imaginable tool of war began to roll off the assembly lines in great numbers as military preparations continued.

Since 1937 Japan had been advancing farther into China. China also badly needed help from the United States. As a result supplies also began to flow to the Far East. The president announced to the world that America was "the arsenal of democracy." With these words, he committed the country to the delivery of more and more guns, planes and ships to America's friends overseas.

A deckload of lend-lease Lockheed A-20 bombers on a merchant ship bound for Europe

Lend-Lease

Until the winter of 1940–1941 Great Britain paid cash for all supplies received from the United States. But wars are expensive, and Great Britain's money was running out. The idea of "lend-lease" had been discussed for some time. In arguing for the idea President Roosevelt stated: "If your neighbor's house is on fire and he needs to use your hose to fight the fire, you give it to him. You don't expect your neighbor to pay you for the hose but merely give it back when the fire is out."

Lend-lease was the same sort of situation. The fires of war were raging in Europe and the Far East. America would lend its friends overseas the supplies to fight their battles. They would pay the U.S. back when they were able.

Congress passed the Lend-Lease Act in March 1941. This act called for providing friendly countries not only with military supplies but also with food. From March 1941 until August 1945 the United States provided over $43 billion in aid to 45 nations at war with Germany, Italy and Japan.

The British in North Africa welcomed these newly delivered Sherman tanks. American lend-lease tanks were badly needed in the desert war against the Italians and Germans.

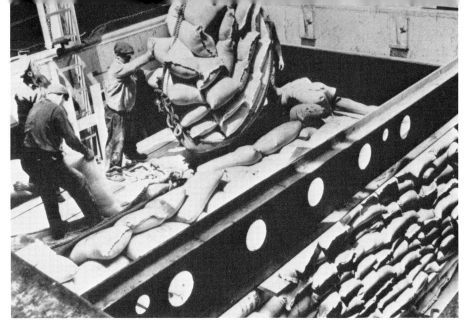

Great Britain had always received a large amount of its food from abroad. When the war started, huge quantities of food had to be delivered by convoys of merchant ships.

In return the United States received "reverse lend-lease." Countries receiving aid gave the U. S. what materials and services they could produce in payment. Sometimes these countries paid by feeding and housing American soldiers stationed on their territory. After the war was over other countries made payments of money to the United States for the lend-lease materials they had received.

On March 29, 1941, President Roosevelt sent a message to Great Britain's Prime Minister Winston Churchill. He stated that the United States was ready to send to England 5,400 airplanes, 400,000 submachine guns, 3,400 trucks, 5,500 anti-aircraft guns, 60 patrol bombing planes and 180 navy fighters.

A good example of how American equipment was put to use is the story of the USS *Buchanan*. A rusty old destroyer was put back in service with the help of American seamen. It was renamed the HMS *Campbelltown.* Armed with guns and ammunition also supplied by America, this gallant old ship carried out a daring raid on the German naval base at Saint-Nazaire, France.

Under cover of darkness, and loaded with tons of high explosives, the *Campbelltown* sailed into Saint-Nazaire harbor. Once inside, the British crew quietly slipped overboard into small boats. Then they set off the explosives and deliberately sank their ship. It blocked the entrance to the harbor so that it could not be used for six months.

Lend-Lease for the Soviet Union

The Soviet Union had joined Germany in the invasion of Poland in September 1939. However, the Germans turned around and attacked the Soviet Union on June 22, 1941. The Soviet Union became one of the Allies. Like Great Britain, it also needed help from the United States. Huge convoys started sailing the North Atlantic, carrying supplies for the Soviets to the far northern port of Murmansk.

A lend-lease locomotive being loaded onto a merchant ship for delivery to Iran. There it would haul needed lend-lease supplies northward to the Soviet Union.

Having lost thousands of aircraft to the German blitzkrieg attacks, the Soviet Union needed replacements badly. At an Iranian airfield, lend-lease A-20 bombers and P-39 and P-40 fighters are assembled and tested by American crews before being turned over to Soviet pilots.

Bad winter weather and active German submarines, surface warships and bombers made that northern route very dangerous. A southern supply route was needed. Convoys had to sail south around Africa and then up through the Indian Ocean. Supplies were landed in Iran. There they were placed on trucks and trains for transport into the Soviet Union..

As part of lend-lease, American ships and crews carried these supplies. American civilians and soldiers helped build and run the railroads in Iran. American mechanics and pilots assembled and tested the military aircraft that had made the long journey by sea from U.S. aircraft factories.

Before America officially entered the war, hundreds of locomotives and thousands of trucks were delivered to the Soviets. Soon tanks and aircraft were arriving by the thousands. The Soviet Union and Great Britain kept the supply lines open while lend-lease funds provided the men and equipment. All of this activity helped Americans get ready for the war they were about to enter.

Chapter 8

LIBERTY SHIPS

   After World War II started in September 1939, German submarine and air attacks sank British naval and merchant ships faster than they could be replaced. British shipyards could not build new vessels or repair damaged ones fast enough. The yards were under constant air attack.

   Still trying to stay out of the European war, the United States had sent most of its navy to the Pacific Ocean. It was headquartered at Pearl Harbor in the Hawaiian Islands. Americans hoped that the Pacific Fleet's presence would keep Japan from starting a war. But as Great Britain's ship losses increased, three American battleships and other, smaller ships were ordered to the Atlantic. The navy command hoped that those ships would not need to fight because they were no match for Germany's most powerful warship, the *Bismarck*.

On the alert for German U-boats, Coast Guard and navy vessels protected convoys bound for England or the Soviet Union while in the western Atlantic Ocean.

Following a miraculous voyage halfway around the world, the badly damaged HMS Illustrious *was repaired — thanks to the U.S. lend-lease ship repair service.*

The larger ships of the U.S. Coast Guard also became part of the Atlantic Fleet to help defend convoys on their way to Great Britain and the Soviet Union. Shipyards in the United States were building new ships and repairing British warships as fast as possible.

The British aircraft carrier HMS *Illustrious,* for example, was severely damaged in battle in the Mediterranean Sea. After making minor repairs to get it sailing again, the ship's crew sailed it through the Suez Canal, and then south around the tip of Africa. From there it sailed north across the Atlantic Ocean to Norfolk, Virginia, where it was repaired and put back into service.

Numerous other Allied vessels were repaired using lend-lease funds. Freighters that had belonged to captured European countries, such as France, Belgium and Norway, came to U.S. ports for service and repair under the lend-lease ship repair program.

But even using every shipyard in the United States, the demand for new ships and repairs could not be met. Something had to be done. America's answer was found in mass production.

Liberty Ships on a stormy sea as they carry supplies to U.S. allies overseas

The Liberty Ship Miracle

The United States had started a major shipbuilding program in 1936. By 1941 over 50 new ships had been built. But they were still not enough. In May 1941 President Roosevelt declared a national emergency. This called for a crash program of merchant and naval shipbuilding.

American shipyards built two very good designs—the British "ocean class" vessels and the American "C" series merchant ships. Ships had always been built one at a time, by hand. The Kaiser Company in California developed an amazing system of mass-producing "Liberty Ships." These were medium-size vessels of 10,000 tons. Kaiser had different sections of a ship built in different locations. The sections were then delivered to a single shipyard where they were joined together. An entire ship was completed faster than ever before.

At the start, 8 to 10 Liberty Ships were delivered each month. Within a couple of years Liberty Ships were being launched at the rate of over 150 ships a month or about 5 ships every 24 hours. Thousands of these and other ships were delivered to the Allies and to the American navy and merchant marine.

To replace the hundreds of Allied merchant ships being sunk, the United States developed the Liberty Ship. Starting in 1941, the Kaiser Company worked day and night to deliver Liberty Ships by the thousands.

Merchant ships in convoy were attacked almost daily during early 1941. Here a U.S. tanker explodes after being torpedoed by a U-boat.

The Ocean War

The United States did not limit its help to producing new ships and making repairs. In 1940 the U.S. Navy patrolled the western Atlantic Ocean. Its job was to look for German U-boats and surface raiders. Any ships that sighted German vessels warned British convoys of possible danger.

At first the navy was not allowed to shoot at German vessels because the United States was not at war. The naval ships could act only as escorts to merchant convoys. Even when lend-lease started, U.S. merchant vessels sailing in convoys to the Soviet Union and to Great Britain were not armed. In order to protect those ships, the U.S. Navy ordered that any German or Italian ship sighted in the western Atlantic was to be followed and sunk.

The U.S. Army also helped to protect the Atlantic. The army set up bases in Greenland and in Newfoundland in Canada. Bases in Greenland were given code names beginning with "Bluie," such as Bluie West One.

However, during 1941 the German navy began to attack every non-German ship it saw. Several American merchant ships were sunk. The lives of merchant sailors were being lost. Americans began to urge Congress to repeal, or cancel, the last part of the Neutrality Act, which kept American merchant ships from being armed.

Then, in October, a German U-boat fired at an American destroyer, the USS *Kearny,* killing several sailors. Twelve days later, another destroyer, the USS *Reuben James*, was also torpedoed, killing 111 men. Congress quickly voted to allow merchant ships to be armed. Convoys could now protect themselves.

The USS Kearny *after a German U-boat attack. Severely damaged, the destroyer is awaiting repairs after making its way to a safe harbor in Iceland.*

Chapter 9

THE FLYING TIGERS

In 1939 the Army Air Corps was equipped with out-of-date aircraft such as Martin B-10 bombers and Curtiss P-26 pursuit-type aircraft. It could not have fought the modern air forces of either Germany or Japan. However, after seeing what was taking place in Europe, the government ordered new long-range bombers and high-speed fighter aircraft.

The first all-new military aircraft to go into mass production was the Curtiss P-40, a fighter plane called the Warhawk. An order was placed for $13 million worth of P-40s in 1939. It was the largest peacetime airplane order ever made in America. When the order was placed, no one knew that it would supply airplanes for a group that would become world famous—the Flying Tigers.

The pre-war Army Air Corps was equipped with outdated planes such as this Curtiss P-26 pursuit-type aircraft. Although skilled and well trained, the air corps pilots were not prepared for a modern war.

Claire Chennault, known as Old Leatherface, retired from the Army Air Corps in 1937. He was immediately hired by the Chinese government to train its air force. In 1941 he formed the Flying Tigers.

Chennault and the Flying Tigers

The Eagle Squadrons served in England. But another group of brave young American pilots went to war in the Far East. This small group was officially known as the American Volunteer Group, but they called themselves the Flying Tigers. They were formed in 1941 at the request of the Chinese government. The group was commanded by a retired U.S. Army Air Corps officer, Claire Chennault.

The Chinese air force had been severely beaten by the Japanese. In 1937 Chennault was hired by the Chinese government to help train its air force. Chennault was one of the world's authorities on modern fighter aircraft. He had studied aerial warfare and fighter tactics for many years while with the U.S. Army Air Corps. He had fought against and observed the Japanese air force in battle.

Flying Tiger ground crews preparing the shark-nosed P-40 fighters for a mission against Japanese bombers. The Flying Tigers flew out of primitive dirt fields in Burma and China.

By 1940 it was clear to Chennault that the Chinese air force needed help badly. After many requests to the United States government, the Chinese were allowed to form the American Volunteer Group. The United States loaned China $100 million to purchase 100 Curtiss P-40 fighter planes and spare parts and to hire and train the pilots and ground crew.

The men of the Flying Tigers were not officially part of the U.S. armed forces. But, with U.S. government permission, all of them were recruited from the army, navy, or marine air forces. The men who decided to join were given honorable discharges and allowed to sign up for duty with the Chinese. They were offered high pay, adventure and possible death. All experience they gained would be shared with the U.S. Army Air Corps.

The Tigers' Mission

By mid-1941 China's seaports had all been captured by the Japanese. Supplies had to be brought into the country through Hanoi, Indochina (now Vietnam) or from Rangoon, Burma. In Burma, goods were carried by train partway. Then they were transferred to trucks to be carried up a mountainous route called the Burma Road. This twisting road ended in Kunming, China. The Flying Tigers' job was to defend these two supply lines.

All the Flying Tiger volunteers were sent to Burma, where Chennault taught them how to fly and fight in the P-40. He taught them all he knew about the Japanese aircraft they would face. Many of the pilots had never flown fighters. Some were injured or killed during training. Dozens of P-40s were wrecked.

An aerial view of the Burma Road as it winds through the mountains of Burma and China. Built mostly by hand by Burmese and Chinese laborers, the road was cut through mountains and trackless jungles.

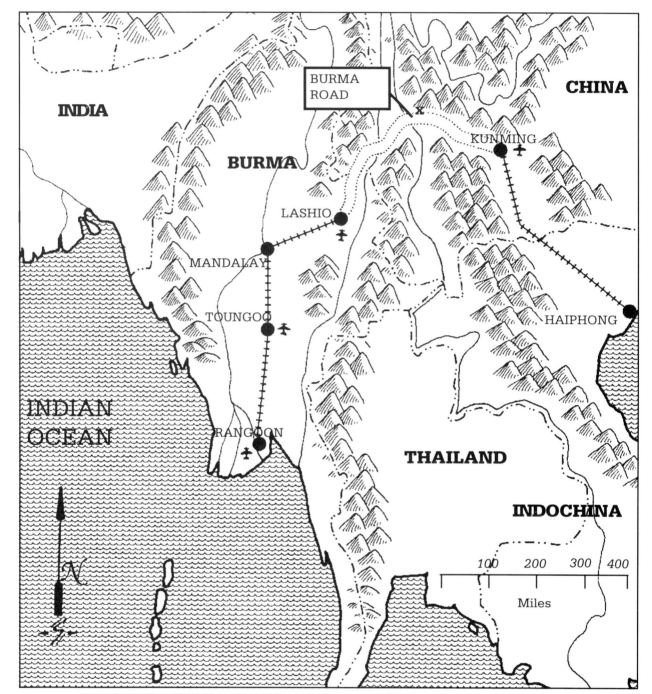

In spring 1941 the railroad from Haiphong to Kunming had been
captured by the Japanese. The Rangoon railroad and the Burma Road
were the main supply routes to China. The Flying Tigers' main task was
to keep the Burma Road safe from Japanese attack. The Flying Tigers
flew out of bases in Rangoon, Toungoo and Lashio, Burma, and from
their main base in Kunming, China.

40

Flying Tiger pilots lined up in front of a shark-nosed P-40 fighter

After six months of training, the volunteers were ready to fight. And then the Japanese bombed Pearl Harbor. Even with the United States officially at war, the Americans of the Flying Tigers were still part of the Chinese air force. They first saw action on December 20, 1941. That day ten Japanese bombers tried to bomb Kunming. The Flying Tigers were waiting above them. They shot down four of the enemy bombers.

During the next six months the Flying Tigers made history in their P-40s, which they painted to look like sharp-toothed sharks. These young men shot down or destroyed on the ground over 350 Japanese fighters and bombers. The Flying Tigers lost only 12 P-40s to enemy action. The whole world watched in amazement as this small group fought the Japanese air force.

On July 4, 1942, the Flying Tigers and the American Volunteer Group came to an end. Colonel Chennault of the

Chinese air force became Brigadier General Chennault of the U.S. Army Air Corps. A number of the pilots and ground crew members were also transferred into the air corps and along with General Chennault stayed in China.

U.S. Air Power

During the years between World War I and World War II the air corps was part of the U.S. Army. It was controlled by ground officers who wanted to use airplanes as if they were artillery—gun platforms in the air. The corps was equipped and trained to fight as it had in World War I. The final role of the modern air force did not develop until after the war in Europe had started.

The United States was fortunate to have been working on two other planes that turned out to be as important as the P-40. Boeing's B-17 Flying Fortress and the B-24 Liberator (built by Consolidated) were long-range bombers with four huge engines. They allowed the air corps to fly long distances to carry out bombing attacks deep in enemy territory. Neither the German nor the Japanese air forces were successful in producing four-engine bombers.

A Liberator that was built for the Royal Air Force in 1940 with lend-lease funds. The U.S. Air Force version was known as the B-24 and was used throughout the war as a long-range bomber.

Newly drafted GIs marching on a wintry day in spring 1941

Canadian and British air crews flew American lend-lease aircraft such as the B-24 from Canada to airfields in the north of England. They flew over part of the world where few navigation aids had ever been built. It was dangerous and difficult to find their way through dense ocean fogs. Also, the pilots and navigators were often inexperienced. Again America was asked to help.

American pilots were given permission to fly airplanes being delivered to Great Britain at least as far as Newfoundland. Airfields were built there as well as at the Bluie bases on Greenland. Radio navigation aids were installed. American civilian pilots were hired to help the British deliver the much-needed aircraft to England. Many Lockheed Hudson bombers and larger bombers and transport aircraft were delivered.

By 1941 when America actually entered the war, there were many pilots ready to go into the Army Air Corps. It became the most powerful air force in the world.

Ready for War

With every passing month, America was building its readiness for war while helping its friends across the oceans. New weapons, ships and aircraft were being manufactured in ever bigger numbers. Millions of men were in training.

Many Americans still thought that the United States would continue to only help Great Britain, the Soviet Union and China. They did not know that they would soon be at war themselves.

But on December 7, 1941, more than two years after the war started in Europe, Japan bombed America's naval base at Pearl Harbor in Hawaii. Within hours, the United States was at war with Japan. Because Germany and Japan were allies, America went to war with Germany too.

Fortunately, America's vast military and industrial might was ready to help its allies. American GIs were prepared to fight the dictators who wanted to take over the world. Within weeks, American soldiers, sailors, aircrews and marines were being sent all over the world.

Because the United States had first helped its friends, the nation was now ready to fight the huge war that everyone hoped would finally make the world safe for democracy.

A smiling President Franklin D. Roosevelt and his wife, Eleanor, during his third inauguration in January 1941. The smiles would disappear when Pearl Harbor was bombed at the end of the year.

Pearl Harbor! This great naval base in the Hawaiian Islands was home for the U.S. Pacific Fleet. There were 94 ships in Pearl Harbor on December 7, 1941. They were stationed there to show the world that the United States was prepared for war. But then, without warning, the Japanese attacked! America was finally at war.

GLOSSARY

Allies The nations that opposed Germany, Japan and Italy during World War II: Great Britain, the United States, France and the Soviet Union.

Army Air Corps The aviation branch of the U.S. Army during World War II. It became the U.S. Air Force in 1947.

barracks Buildings used to house people in the military.

blitzkrieg "Lightning war," in German.

convoy A group of merchant or military ships sailing together with navy escorts for protection.

Depression The years from 1929 to 1939, marked by business and bank failures, high unemployment and falling prices.

draftee A person whose name has been drawn for possible military service.

GI Any man in military service during World War II; short for Government Issue.

induction The act of actually being taken into military service.

isolationist A person who believes his or her country should remain apart from the problems of other nations.

lend-lease Military and non-military supplies provided by the United States to the Allies during the war.

merchant marine Non-military ships and shipping.

Nazi A member of the National Socialist party that ruled Germany from 1933 to 1945 under Adolf Hitler.

neutral Not taking sides in other nations' wars.

pacifist A person who is against war for any reason.

recruit A volunteer or draftee joining a military unit.

RAF The Royal Air Force of Great Britain.

sabotage A destructive act by an enemy against military or non-military installations during a time of war.

Selective Service Required military service, or the "draft."

swastika The four-branched symbol that represents Nazi Germany.

Treaty of Versailles The treaty signed at the end of World War I.

U-boat A German submarine; short for *untersee-boot*, or undersea boat.

INDEX